I0156636

PREPARED FOR PUBLICATION
BY
HISTORIC PULISHING

ISBN-13:
978-1946640406

ISBN-10:
1946640409

HISTORIC PULISHING
©2017 (Edited Materials)

The American Telescope
With
An Appeal to Backslidden Christians

Collaboratively Written

By

Joshua Lawrence
[1778-1843]

And

Theo Whitfield
[1834-1894]

PHILADELPHIA
PRINTED FOR THE AUTHOR.
1825.

PART 1

The American Telescope,
by a Clodhopper, of North Carolina
By
Joshua Lawrence

THE AMERICAN TELESCOPE,

BY
A CLODHOPPER,
OF
NORTH CAROLINA.

Written
By
Joshua Lawrence

Edited
By J. Mitchell

PHILADELPHIA;
PRINTED FOR THE AUTHOR.
1825.

The American Telescope

THE
AMERICAN TELESCOPE.

IT is now about fifteen years since the Missionary cause was introduced into North Carolina, with great show of zeal, and love for the poor Indians on our continent. Their deplorable condition was depicted in the liveliest colors, and with all that sympathy and apparent feeling for their poor lost souls, calculated to soften a heart of stone, and awaken in the coldest-hearted Christian, the most earnest emotions for their salvation. However, there was something then, and ever has been, that I dreaded as a viper full of deadly poison. Although it was glossed over with the love of souls; the worth of souls; starving souls for want of knowledge, &c. &c. with all the embellishments of fine language, and great talents in teaching; added to which, were many tears, much show of feeling, and semblance of Christian sincerity; yet I

11

could not help being filled with a jealousy, that there was death in the pot.--And I have stood as an opposer and observer ever since, and now offer the public a few thoughts, and hazard some conjectures, on the future consequences of the Missionary and other societies, abounding in our land of freedom.

In the first place, several associated bodies proceeded to appoint delegates; say, four or five from each of their respective bodies, to form a convention or Missionary board, to lay a plan for the conversion of the heathen; (for no man could be found among all the seeming feeling ones for poor Indian souls, that would comply with the command of Christ: to take neither gold, nor silver, nor scrip; neither two coats; and go into all the world and preach the gospel to every creature, without money or price.)--These delegated divines, therefore, met together at ----, to hold the mighty council, to form the benevolent plan of converting the Indians, quickly. And what is the result of their deliberations on so important a subject? Why, money! money! Let the people give us of their money, and the mighty work can be done. What? men do the work with money, which none but God can do by his grace and spirit! Folly indeed-- but the plan was drawn, and this is as near the spirit and principle of it, as I am able to describe--

First: We must take all possible care to make the case of the Indians as bad as we can. Secondly: We must show with great zeal, how much our hearts feel, by affectation only, since we are not willing to go ourselves; and if need should so require to get a little more money, we must shed some tears before our congregations. Thirdly: Our Missionary texts must be well chosen and pathetically handled, to excite the sympathy of our hearers, and open their hearts to the Indians; and then while they are in that soft state, let a collection be made, and we shall draw plentifully from their pockets. Fourthly: Let various societies be formed, to take in members at one or two dollars a year, for membership; and have so much at one time to constitute one a member or a director for life, and this will greatly contribute to our getting money. Fifthly: Let us create titles, such as presidents, vice-presidents, corresponding secretaries, and treasurers, in these new societies, with boards of directors, and other unheard of titles of honor in the New Testament; and this will be a good bait; since men delight to be honored, and have their names carried abroad, and no doubt cause many to do much in aiding our schemes of getting money. Sixthly: Let travelling beggars be appointed, crying wherever they go--give! give us of your money to convert the heathen. How unlike the prophets, John the Baptist, Jesus Christ, the apostles, a Luther, a George Whitfield, a Wesley, a Dow, and a thousand others, who are ornaments to the free gospel of Christ; all impressed with the worth of souls; and who go forth taking up their cross, denying themselves, and devoting themselves to the work of God, for the good of men: dependent on God, without begging or being shamefully backed by monied societies.

By hard squeezing, somewhere about seven hundred and fifty dollars was collected, and deposited with Mr. Treasurer, until further orders from this board of wise divines, and set of new schemers in gospel theory. They met, and met again, from year to year, to re-organize their plan of money getting. Some years after, out comes a shameful Circular from this wise board, (when they had found out they were but men,) that if any man that

15

had given, wanted his money back, he could have it, by applying; but that they were persuaded better things of of them that had given; (a proof of their vanity and folly; for they now plead the hostility of the Indians, and want of proper persons to teach school, &c. &c.) Soon the great and mighty institutions of foreign and domestic missions, with bible societies and theological seminaries, were circulated, with all the high encomiums that the English language could furnish; and into them, they and their perverted funds began to fall. Now, in this mighty field to do wonders, in sending the gospel to the destitute at home and abroad, to work this wise board of directors go, with redoubled ardour, setting the wisdom of all their heads to work, to invent new plans of getting more money-- and how they may, by the by, handle a little of the precious stuff themselves, I shall here notice, as the people seem to bleed pretty freely.

And so, Seventhly: While in council they make a bargain, you comb my head, and I will scratch your back;--you confer on me the honorable title of gospel beggar or missionary hireling, at one dollar and twenty-five cents per day, or forty dollars per month, if you think I have a good talent for begging; or I will beg for you, if you will pay me for my services; or I will play into your hands, if you will play into mine--share the profits. Cheat and fleece the people out of their hard earnings, upon condition you will let me beg in the name of your honorable society; for I am ashamed to beg for myself, lest the people raise the hue and cry--money hunter, &c.

What abominable hypocrisy! If the cause espoused be holy, just, virtuous and honorable, why not come openly out to the world, and tell the congregations that you have been hired by the board of domestic or foreign missions, for one dollar and twenty five cents per day, to beg for them; and that the beggar and the board are to divide the money, and all over wages is to be saved for other hirelings, doctors, and reverends; then congregations would know how to act, and such characters act more worthy the Christian minister and honest man.

Eighthly: The sound destitute, destitute, destitute places of the gospel, must re-echo in all our churches, to work upon our hearers to get more money in our exhausting coffers, and keep our fingers greased; for who can go without a fine coat and plenty of money! And where have domestic missionaries gone? Have they gone to the most destitute parts of North Carolina, and other places? No. Believe me--these hirelings like to be fed on better fare than the poor can give them--they like the houses of colonels, squires, and to have very rich and fat tables and stables, where their horses will be well provided for; and to ride good roads: in short, the main point is to go about towns, and to the richest churches and neighborhoods, where the most money is to be begged:--and their conduct proves it, with all their pretense of the love of souls. I wish, indeed, that money may not make the preacher go, as well as the mare.

These beggars keep a mighty cry about the destitute. Why not go to them, if their hearts are so affected about their condition, and then we shall have cause to say, souls, and not money, is their object. But they tell us, money is wanting; and when they have begged enough, then they are going to send preachers to the destitute. How much will be enough? They have had their thousands, and I do not yet see that the destitute places in North Carolina are a whit the better supplied; and I doubt whether they would be, if the benevolent public were to give thousands more. The beggars, in all probability, would still get the greatest part, for riding where they could sell, what they call gospel, to the highest bidder, and find the most money.--The conduct of some, in several instances, has proved the fact, that money was the main object. For as soon as they had got that, they have bid the churches farewell, and gone to see where they could find more.

But who are they going to send, when they get money enough? Why, say they, "men of God." That is a mistake; God's ministers are not hirelings; they do not divine for money, like Balaam, nor run up and down the country, hired, this way and that way, as the current of gain shifts. Nor are they anxious, like Judas, to have the bag, and receive their thirty pieces of silver. In this text, we see the character of a minister of God:

"Feed the flock of God, over which the Holy Ghost has made you overseers; taking the oversight thereof willingly, and of a ready mind, and not for filthy lucre's sake." But if they send ministers at all to the destitute, they will send hirelings, Judases or Balaam's. For if they will not go for the love of God and the good of souls, but you must give them money to make them move, I contend, that money is the main spring of action-- the great wheel that gives motion to their going. The sake, is filthy lucre or money, since no sake could move them but money sake. Furnish money, and what crowds are moving in every direction, hunting money, fortunes, and places of profit. Stop the money, and you would see a squandering among these Judases at once. But, you would see God's ministers, like regular stars, moving each one in his own sphere, with his work before him, feeding the flock with life, enduring poverty and everything else, if need be, for the cause of God, and the souls of men.--In a word, like the prophets and apostles, stemming every opposition; and counting everything but loss, so that they can win souls to Christ.

The true ministers of Christ are always more ready to give, than receive. But the men sent out by missionary boards, in this day, will be only a curse, instead of a blessing, to God's Israel. Their discourses, generally, are without life or substance, and are a burthen to the godly. And they squint an eye to a purse, with as much intenseness as ever Eve did at the forbidden fruit.

Some great writer has said, this is an age of wonders; and I begin to think it is so indeed; for the idea I used to entertain of beggars, was, that they were poor, decripped, ragged, helpless beings, destitute of the means of supporting themselves. But how wonderfully times have changed; for now we see hearty, hale men, and young men in the prime and vigour of life, clothed in the finest black and blue broad cloth, with fur hats, boots, spurs, silk jackets, silver tipped bridles and stirrups, watches, &c. &c. turned beggars--great beggars. They tell us, they beg for the sake of Christ and the heathen; but fortunately for us all, these fellows cannot keep the eat in the wallet; for one of these northern beggars, not long since, passed through North Carolina, and being asked how much he had collected, he said about two thousand dollars. Moreover, pray, sir, said the inquirer, what per centum do they give you for begging? He said his fees would come to about four hundred dollars. And pray, sir, are you a preacher too: said the inquirer, looking gravely in his face? O yes! said he, I attempt to preach as I go--hanging down his head, and throwing his fine broad cloth legs over each other, and twisting his watch key. Yes, and I think, said the man, a great many of you had better be at work, than going about in the garb of a preacher, as you pretend, begging the poor laborers for their money; for you look more like a doctor, or a young lawyer, with your frizzled foretop and fine clothing, than a preacher. In addition, I suppose, the North Carolinians might have went to hell for your preaching, if it had not been for the four hundred dollars you expected to get. No, he replied, I don't know that I should have come, but the society hired me to come, and I must live somehow; and you'll give something, will you not? No, that I won't, said the man. If I have got anything to give, I will give it to our old preacher, who will preach whether we pay him or not; and not to such fellows as you, who are riding about dressed up in your fine broad cloth, hunting a rich wife, and begging money; while I must wear my old tow trousers, and work in the hot sun to maintain such fellows. No, that I won't, repeated the man. O yes! but you can, I know, and will give me something, continued the beggar. I will not, was the reply.

These beggars are like hungry mosquitoes--knock them off, and they will at you again, and again, until they suck your money, if possible. Say, and prove, if any man can, that there is one trait of true apostolic character in these fellows, and the controversy will be at an end. Their love of money has betrayed them, as it did Simon Magus. Sent out by missionary boards, and not by Jesus Christ, they look for profit by fleecing the people; lugging the cause of God, and the care of the heathen in, to aid them in getting money.

Another deep-laid scheme to get money, is, to draw up the most affecting and sympathetic addresses, to publish in their circulating reports, in which the very bowels of antiquity are often ransacked, to get something that may touch the feelings of the community; for no other purpose, but to get their money. A combination of the best talents are employed to form one of these Circulars, which, at best, to say no worse of them, are nothing but money speculations, human contrivances, and pompous expressions, to deceive the hearts of the simple, and live on their spoil.

Some thousands have been sent to India, to support the lovers of money there, and turn that land of heathenism into a Paradise of saints. And what has been done there? What mighty works have been wrought by all the hundreds of thousands of dollars that have been expended, and all the numerous missionaries that have been sent, from this and other countries! I have heard, as with the trumpet's fame, that about three hundred persons have been, at last, persuaded to renounce cast and turn Christian, after fifteen or twenty years' labor; when a single Peter, a Paul, a Luther, a Whitfield, a Wesley, and others, being sent of God, have done more in a few days or weeks, without the aid of self-created societies, and monied institutions, and numerous beggars not sanctioned by the word of God, nor found in the pages of the New Testament. As the churches in this country are now going on, they will soon be no better than the church of Rome, and the High Church of England; for money and titles have always been the object of Popes and Popish priests, and also of the clergy of the Church of England, who once had the command of sixteen thousand weight of tobacco, annually, in this country, to turn into money. Titles and money have always corrupted the ministry, and they have already began to disgrace it in North Carolina. The same causes will always produce like effects; and let the true children of God watch and beware.

But to quiet our fears, and make us tamely acquiesce, while the "reverend" clergy cut the strings of our purses, and put the yoke of tyranny snug on our necks, they tell us the mind of God is with his people. If they were to tell me the mind of the devil was with many in this day, who profess to be his servants, I could readily believe it. Can the mind of God be, where the whole soul is engaged in schemes to get money!! Look and see, if you find such a spirit with the prophets, John the Baptist, and the apostles. No, indeed! But be still, say they; this is the way God is about to usher in the glorious millennium. Rather, I say, it is the way that the devil will soon triumph over all true religion, and aggrandize his transformed ministers, and make them pensioners of state. Money and education are power; and in the management of skillful hands, great effects may, in a short time, be produced.

Can one instance be shown, from the first of Genesis to the last of the Revelation, where God has ever made money a means of spreading his religion? Has it not been done by humble and unostentatious persons, specially chosen of God, without any call for money? Look at a Jonah, Peter, Paul, and Barnabas, all sent on special missions. We hear nothing of money or backing societies, before they can go: but now thousands must be had on hand, and good promises for more of the precious stuff, before our missionaries can move a peg. And I leave the reader to judge, what side such missionaries belong to.

But it seems that the mind of God is not always with his people, much less, with those that call themselves his people, but are in reality the devil's people; or if the devil does not personally preside in the chair as president, yet he votes in the voters, and that is as good, and much better; because, he acts in the back ground, unsuspected; and you shall see who turns the wheel.

Was the mind of God with the great Baptist Association of Virginia, when they created Samuel Harris Apostle of Virginia? Did not the devil turn the wheel there? We laugh at the folly now, of that set of wise ministers; and so will posterity, in years to come, at all the unscriptural works of darkness now going on, where the devil turns the wheel. And who can help thinking the devil turns the wheel, where money is but too plainly seen to be the object of each and every movement.

Was the mind of God with his church and people of Israel, at the foot of Mount Horeb, when the people said to that great saint, Aaron: "Come make us gods to go before us into Egypt; for as for this Moses, we wist not what has become of him:"--and gave him their gold, jewels and bracelets, of which he made the idol calf; and kicked up such a mighty dust, dancing around the god of their own making.

Was the mind of God with his people, when Jeroboam made the two golden calves, and set one in Dan and the other in Bethel, and said, "these are thy gods O Israel?" Rather, does it not show the consequences of the Church of God being connected with the great men of this world; for then the devil will be sure to turn the wheel. And while our Missionary, bible, and tract societies, and theological schools, are connected with the men of this world, the devil is sure to turn the wheel, and give the casting vote in his favor.

Was the mind of God with the church at Corinth, when they perverted the right use of the Lord's supper?

Was the mind of God with the church of Rome, when they began to create titles, bishops, cardinals, arch-bishops, universal bishop, sovereign pontiff, Christ's vicar, prince of the apostles, &c. &c.--These measures were as innocent, I conceive, in their first appearance, as presidents, vice-presidents, corresponding secretaries, recording secretaries, board of directors, &c. which are all unscriptural titles, names and offices, unbecoming God's people.

And where did these titles lead to in the end? Why they came up to our lord god the Pope, sovereign Pontiff over the whole world; having the keys of heaven, hell, and purgatory; and whoever would go in, must pay toll to his holiness the Pope, and bow to what he thought right, or enter the hellish inquisition, and suffer death in the most horrid forms. All this was brought about by getting off gospel ground, under the show of religion,

out of the warrant of the New
Testament. Shall we not then take
care of those innocent things you call
titles, the corrupters of the Church of
God. These are the scorpions that
have stings in their tails, and have
stricken thousands to ruin. Oh ye sons
of Columbia! stand up and look round
yourselves; and behold what strides
are making by an ever-busy clergy, to
forge the chains of tyranny for your
bodies and consciences! Be alarmed,
before your necks are in the yoke--for
these things must come in side-ways,
or as an entering wedge; and one step
off from gospel ground, gives room
for another, until death is in the pot,
and the devil at the wheel.

Was the mind of God with his
people, when the dissenting clergy
from popery in England, appointed
king Henry head of the Church, and
parliament the guardians of its
affairs!! See what followed:
persecution, religious taxation, fines

and imprisonment throughout England--the clergy prompting those in power, to do these things for their own gain. Surely the devil turned the wheel, and voted in the voters. And does it not show us, as a beacon, on our own coast, how we should endeavor to keep the Church apart from any influence of the men of this world; for they know not the things of the spirit; and hence their influence is always bad. But the clergy want to get hold of their fat purses, and this is the way they have taken to do it: to build a sort of National Church, and let them come into it for pay; having a fixed price for members, directors, and presidents for life; and so

they make a sort of half-brothers of the governors and rich men of this world.

As for God's putting it in the hearts of his people to go this way to work to convert the world, it is what I cannot yet believe. For God cannot change, nor do I think he will change his plan of carrying on his work;--and what monied institutions and societies do we find, supporting the prophets among the Jews;--or what self-created bodies for obtaining money, backed the apostles and first preachers of the gospel? Let some example, or authority, be shown from the word of God, if it can be. The authority of men will not answer for me, in a business of such importance. Give me--thus saith the Lord, or else give up the point.

Did monied societies support the Reformers? No; they hazarded all, and suffered the loss of all things for the sake of Christ. Hence we see, that this modern practice of spreading religion by means of money, and monied societies, is neither sanctioned by the word of God, nor the example of the prophets, the apostles, or the reformers; but well agrees with the Church of Rome, and high Church of

England. The cry of money, money, is heard throughout the Church of Rome, from the pope to the friar; and in the Church of England, from the bishop down to the warden constable.

Has God, after four thousand years, changed his plan of carrying on his work? Or has He lately seen that monied institutions are necessary means for converting the world? Certainly not, but the Lord's way of carrying on his work, does not suit men of high minds, who want to be gods themselves, and wrest from his hands the power of making Christians in his own way; and prescribe paths for Jehovah to walk in that may please themselves, and the men of this world. Where, in all the Scriptures, shall we find any self-created societies, and monied institutions, to advance the cause of true religion! And if they cannot be found there, a man must be blind not to see that they are mere human inventions; and that the devil is turning the wheel; and will only corrupt the Church, and make mankind more degenerate and wicked.

Monied institutions have supported the Church of Rome, and high Church of England, in their thirst for aggrandizement, and to lord it over the consciences of men. But dissenters, in no age, until of late, or about a century, have needed any such support. As for the Gospel, one of its chief glories is, that it stands on the arm of Omnipotence, and commends itself to the consciences of men-- making its way through the kingdoms of this world, in spite of all opposition. Though the heathen rage, and kings, and governors, and rulers of this world, have stood up against the Gospel and God's anointed, and have employed prisons, gibbets, flames, and death, in all their torturing forms, yet have they not prevailed.

And how is it, that the rulers of this world, and the rich, and noble of the earth, who have in all ages opposed the Gospel, and voted against it, have now become its votaries and supporters!! I would as soon believe that the devil is turned a saint at last, as to believe this thing--that human nature should be so changed without a work of grace upon the heart. The truth lies here; the men of this world have always been willing to support that which was called Gospel, or a form of religion, but not the thing itself; for that they hate, and have in all ages of the world. To support the mere form of religion, or a false religion, corrupt men have always been ready enough. Witness their readiness to support idolatry--to support the See of Rome--the Crusades! the Pagan--Mahometan, and all such false and formal religions! Witness how zealous the Pharisees were to support their forms of error, and the traditions of the elders, at the expense of the blood of Christ and his apostles! Witness the Pagan emperors, putting hundreds of thousands to death, to support their absurd Paganism! Witness the high church of England, and church of Rome, destroying and persecuting the most pious in their borders, to support a form of godliness of their own invention, suited to the taste of corrupt lords, dukes, kings, queens, and emperors! Can I, with all these truths before me, and many more, believe that the pompous proceedings, and monied schemes of the present day, are of God!! It is only because the devil is in all these schemes and inventions, that his children support them, and honor them with their presence and approbation. This one circumstance is sufficient to convince me that these great works are not of God, and will only prove an injury to the cause of true religion.

It is certain, that all the pomp and show we now see, for promoting the Lord's work, will at last be brought to naught; because it is not the way of God's choosing. And he will clear all this rubbish away, and afterwards work in his own way, and by instruments of his own choice. For our Lord saith, "marvel not that the world hate you; for you know it hated me before it hated you. It hateth me, because I testify the deeds thereof are evil." What then! do natural men support him and his cause, when they have hated him and his cause in all ages? How inconsistent in itself! It is supporting the thing in appearance only, or that which has a show of the cause of Christ, but which, in reality, is the devil's cause in masquerade. And this has been the manner of the devil, from the days of Cain, down to Constantine the Great; to set up a form of religion, in opposition to the true religion by grace and faith, and maintain it in the world, by men of this world; condemning, killing, and destroying, by a thousand infernal tortures, all the children of God that oppose it. But, in the days of Constantine, he seems to have come to his senses; and, as if he saw, that the massacre of millions could not stop the progress of the religion of Jesus Christ; or, as if gorged with blood, or satisfied with cruelty, he comes to a cessation of arms, all on a sudden; and sits still, as an idle spectator, for a good while. During this time, Constantine repeals all persecuting laws, and then establishes religion by law; honoring the ministers of the Gospel--giving them salaries, and making everything in religion grand, rich and pompous.

But how soon does the devil improve on this plan, and turn all into show and form again;--and then follows persecution of the saints; which has shown itself more or less in every country throughout

Christendom. In England, though they cast off the cruel yoke of Popery, yet they set up the idol of uniformity; manifesting the same persecuting spirit, and contending, by kings, queens, lords of parliament, magistrates, and constables, for the support of a form of godliness, and will-worship; at the same time, opposing the Gospel in its purity and simplicity; and fining and imprisoning those who adhered to it. How dangerous then is a form of religion, armed with the civil power! and how dangerous to trust a body of learned and monied clergy, with any kind of power. Our fathers, who composed the convention to form the Constitution of the State of North Carolina, knew the danger of these men; therefore, inserted an article that no minister of the Gospel, having the cure of souls, should have a seat in either house of the Legislature. They had tasted the gall and venom of this tribe of money-getting characters, and therefore, guarded against them in that article. And if it were not for this article, we should see them electioneering, this way and that way, to get into the Legislature. And could they once obtain an ascendency in the government, they would ride roughshod over the consciences and property of the people, like all other tyrants. There would be no danger in letting the good become members, but to keep out the bad and designing, our fathers thought best to keep all out-- and they were right.

It has been said, that money and education are power. And does not money and education fill the offices of state? Does not money and education levy war, and carry it on? What would America have done in the revolution, had it not been for her wise counselors, continental money, and the silver crowns of France! And what would the missionary societies do for runners and beggars, if it were not for money! What would the Pope of Rome have done for priests to carry about his indulgences and pardons to sell, had it not been for money, a part of which went to pay the priests for their trouble, and the balance was for the Pope to carry on his schemes. It is just so with many of our modern priests: money causes them to go about; a part of what they get they have for begging; and the balance is for the Board of Directors to carry on their plans and schemes. And what they will do in the end, time only can reveal. We see them now making mighty strides in every part of the union, to get hold of money, and what new tricks and schemes are to be played under the mask of religious benevolence to attain something out of view, and not heretofore known in the devil's politics, is left wholly to conjecture.

I have been told of late, the Baptists were like Israel without a king. Now the Israelites desired Samuel to ask the Lord to give them a king that they might be like the nations around them, and have a great man to fight their battles and go in and out before them, but some of our modern Baptists are not so condescending to God as Israel was, to ask of him a great man, or men to go before them; or agreeably to the words of Christ, "pray to the Lord of the harvest to send out more laborers into his vineyard;" but to be like the Church of England, and the Presbyterians around them, they have without any authority from the Lord, set up a priestly polishing machine at headquarters, to polish over young men, and make great ministers of them, to fight their battles and go in and out before them. Are they afraid to trust their cause with God any longer, and so have rejected him after enjoying his protection such a length of time, and will they now depend on an arm of flesh?

The Church of Rome, and other churches, tried the experiment of making great-learned divines, and soon these great divines, bishops, parsons, curates and friars, must have great salaries, and be maintained in high dignity by the people. And so it will be with these young doctors from headquarters, after going through the polishing machine; for, work they cannot, though they will not be ashamed to beg, since it has become fashionable for divines in broad cloth to follow this trade. I should like to know how many we have among us that would rather go to doctor Greatman for instruction, than to Jesus Christ, and would prefer to show themselves approved men for talents and learning, than study to show themselves approved of God for a holy, pious, humble life; or diligence in the ministry, knowledge of the holy Scriptures, having their ministry written on the tables of many hearts--by the power of the spirit of

God attending their unpolished discourses, to the salvation of men!

If what I hear be true, that there are about twelve thousand in all the various polishing machines in this country, preparing themselves to hunt fortunes, live without work, and to please the world, and these like devouring locusts, are soon to be let loose, flying to the most populous towns and cities, and looking about in every hole and corner of the union, where the fattest purse is to be had; in order to live on the labors of others, in pomp and style--for one, I pray, they may keep away from North Carolina; for we have fortune hunters and beggars enough already, who produce disputes, jars and discord among brethren of the same church, if we refuse to give, and are unwilling to be stripped of our hard earnings; while our every day, but faithful and humble ministers, are neglected, and can scarcely procure decent clothing, and provide the necessaries of life for themselves and families.

But we are told by some of our doctors and reverends, that they do not undertake to make ministers out of any sort of men;--that they do not think to change the heart, or call any one to the ministry. This, they let us know, they leave for God to do; while their machine is for giving the last polish--the finishing touch to their qualifications; which operation, is considered far superior, to enable them to please men, than anything God has done to them, or can be expected to do. Now, in the name of the best of causes, and for its sake, I ask them, to give me example or precept from the word of God, or show any of the prophets, John the Baptist, or any of the apostles, who, after being called of God to their respective missions, that ever went to school, or to study under Dr. Greatman, in order to learn how to preach, or what to preach! No example or precept from the word of God, can be produced in support of such a practice; and it is evident, that these theological schools, or machines for polishing ministers, are the inventions of the devil, who is working in the back ground, to undermine the Church of God, and corrupt the ministry and society in general, and fill the world with oppression, wretchedness, and misery.

Look, and see, among the prophets and apostles, whether the Lord had such respect to education and learning! What sort of men did he choose, for the most part, to preach his gospel? and what sort of men has he chosen, in all ages of the Church, to declare his counsel unto men? Peter, John, and all the apostles, Paul excepted, were unlearned and unlettered men; yet, Christ made this no bar, hindrance, or disqualification, to their being his apostles; and generally, in all ages of the Church, God has chosen the poor and unlearned to preach his word; and made them mighty, through grace, to the pulling down of the strong holds of Satan's kingdom; in order, that the power might be of God, and not of men. This cannot be denied; yet our doctors of divinity are trying to pervert the order of God, or help him to finish the work of qualifying ministers. Hear Paul's observations on ministers, &c. "God hath chosen the foolish things of the world, to confound the wise; and the weak things of the world, the base, the despised, and things which are not, hath God chosen:" for what? that no flesh should glory in his presence. And these observations agree with God's conduct in the choice of ministers in all ages, except in a few cases. But our wise and learned doctors, have found out a more excellent way, they think, than God's way;--they are going to instruct and polish numerous young men for the ministry. They may ruin them, but they cannot better them, unless it be to please men. To better them, to please God or profit his church and people, they cannot. For preaching is a gift--the gift of God; and what doctors of divinity are not able to give.

I do not think myself guilty of a breach of religious charity, in saying, that these polishing machines, lately established for qualifying young men to preach, are of the devil, and from high-minded men, who want to maintain their cause by human strength, and an arm of flesh. These high-minded doctors seem, indeed, to me, like some men, who dislike their Maker's work, in making the handsome and elegant horse. Say some, his ears are too long--they must be cropt;--say others, his tail hangs too much down,--he must be nicked before he can please us: and to work, they go, to better the Creator's work, or to make a horse to their own liking. Just so with our learned doctors: after God has converted and called a poor young man to the ministry, and furnished him with every needful qualification, and directed him to go and preach his gospel, it will not answer--he does not please the doctors--he does not speak grammar, nor is he eloquent enough to command the respect of the people. He is not even polite in his manners, and does not know how to conduct himself properly in genteel company. He must be altered before he will answer for a preacher, or be able to please the people, and obtain a salary. Thus the proud and high minded of this world, have, in all ages, set at naught God's ministers, and have heaped up to themselves teachers, having itching ears, who have sounded forth their own praise, and had an eye to the purse.

But God's ministers seek not to go forth in the excellency of speech, and of man's wisdom; for they know that the wisdom of this world is foolishness with God, and they wish to speak as of the ability which God giveth them. But something of the hands of man must be on ministers in this day, before they can preach to please; and to work doctors go, to make them more than God has thought proper to do. Thus they become deformed and disfigured; first, by cropping their long ears of humility in dress and manners, and giving them a proud, dressy carriage, and the polite manners of a young lawyer--which in a minister of the humble Jesus, is more offensive to the pious, than the vilest reptile. Secondly, they learn them to run straight for the purse; and, where the most money and the largest salaries are to be got. Thirdly, they learn them to speak in high flown words, and pompous expressions, so that the poor and unlearned are not able to understand them; and thus they become as barbarians to them that hear. Fourthly, they are made to despise the poor, of which class they once were, before made gentlemen, fortune-hunters, &c. Fifthly, all equality among ministers is destroyed; and, at length, none must be allowed to preach at all, unless they are learned men: and thus the apostles will be put in the back ground, as well as most of God's ministers, and the devil will bear the chief sway in all the churches. Then, all who live godly in Christ Jesus, will suffer persecution, as in former times; for, unregenerate and high minded priests, have been the greatest persecutors of the righteous in every age of the world.

When doctors and reverends saunter, and hanker about state legislators, members of congress, and fawn on governors, and chief men of state, cringing and begging, it is time for Americans to look out. They are not walking in the footsteps of the Apostles, but are seeking their own ends; and are endeavoring to bring together church and state. Nay, it seems, this unnatural connexion is now begun, if we look at the minutes of the Missionary, Tract, Bible and Theological Education Societies, and see whose names are there enrolled as donors, officers, &c. &c.

The Emperor Constantine, and his men of state, with the clergy's juggling together, produced the devil in the end, though all was fair weather at first, as it is now among us. But storms gathered, and at length burst forth in fury and destruction to the people of God. The kings of England, parliament, and the clergy, began to play into each other's hands--and what has been the effect? Let us beware of new and unscriptural projects.--Look at Peter the Hermit, in rags. running bare-foot from city to city, preaching up the crusades, or holy wars as they were termed-- drawing kingdoms into this popular scheme, and causing the destruction of about thirteen thousand lives in this foolish new project. What destruction is witnessed, when church and state meet together! Look at the priests in France, with crucifixes in their hands, encouraging the bloodthirsty Catholics in the murder of sixty thousand Protestants in a night! Look at the Pope of Rome, sending his priests to Baptise at the point of the sword; and, because the Welchmen refused, slaughtered them by thousands! Look at king George, sending his learned priests into this country, and fixing a salary on them of sixteen thousand pounds of tobacco a year, to maintain them in idleness, luxury and pride! Look at the whippings and imprisoning's of the Baptists, in Virginia, and other states, by means of these same well fed priests! Money and learning out of their proper place, or improperly used, corrupt the church and ministry of God. And these corrupting societies overturn any government, however strong its foundation may be at first laid. Because, there is a combination of talents, interest and party spirit; which if strong enough, will prevail over all impediments, destroy liberty of conscience, establish its own power, and fill the land with oppression, wretchedness and misery. Money is a good thing--education is a good thing--power is a good thing--law is a good thing--and death is a good thing--but, they must all stand in their proper place--be used by a proper hand--regulated by a right spirit, and for a right end; else they become scourges of the worst kind to human beings.

It is deemed proper to state, that the author of the foregoing pages is a member of the Baptist Church, in

North Carolina, in very respectable standing. This statement, however, is made, without the knowledge or consent of the writer.

PART 2

An Appeal to Backslidden Christians

By

Theo Whitfield 1834-1894

AN APPEAL
TO
BACKSLIDDEN CHRISTIANS.

BY REV. THEO. WHITFIELD OF MISS.

"Return thou backsliding Israel."--Jer. iii: 12.

Are you not a Christian? Then why is it you live so unlike a Christian? Have you not been redeemed from death by the precious blood of Christ? Have you not been made a citizen of heaven, a son of the Great King and a joint heir with the Lord Jesus? Then why do you live so unlike such an one? Why do unclean words fall from your lips? Why are sinful actions found in your hands? Why are unholy thoughts cherished in your heart? You are ashamed to be called by the name of Christ; I pray God He may not be ashamed to call you by that name in the day of judgment. Let me appeal to you, O backslider. Return to a consistent Christian life. Take up the cross, and "walk worthy of the vocation wherewith you are called."

1. Let your mind revert to the time when first you perceived yourself in the horrible pit of sin exposed to all the curses

of God's Law and to the fiery vengeance of the wrath to come. You deserved to die, and a portion with the devil and his angels was justly allotted to you. In such a miserable plight, felt and acknowledged by yourself, did Christ offer himself through the gospel even to you, saying "Come unto me all ye that labor and are heavy laden and I will give you rest. Take my yoke upon you and learn of me for I am meek and lowly in heart, and ye shall find rest unto your souls." Matthew ii: 28, 29. This offer you embraced, in it you confided, and from it your heart drew hope and joy, Christ had therein promised to save you. But what did you promise to Him? Was it not to wear His yoke and receive His commandments? Far it be from me to say that because of your promise to be His servant, He saved you, that because you gave yourself to, He gave Himself to you, or that when you cast off His yoke, He also cast you from His grace. But if you have indeed embraced Him as your Savior, you did at the same time embrace His cross and covenanted to carry it so long as you should live. And oh! how have you kept that covenant! What yoke are you now wearing but that of sin? What commandments do you keep save the rude promptings of your own passions or the demands of a sinful world? How much more careful are you not to break friendship with your sin loving companions than not to wound your Savior friend? How much more anxious not to sacrifice the good opinion of the world than not to sacrifice your faith plighted to Christ! How much more ready to indulge your unworthy passions than dare to serve your Redeemer! Do you esteem the most sacred of all vows? Then remember those which you made to Christ when you committed your soul to Him, as your only Savior. Then He rescued you from the jaws of Hell and adopted you into the family of heaven--will you not keep vows with Him? His mercy is now your only possible salvation--will you not keep vows with Him? He only can be your intercessor with God, your Advocate in the Judgment and your friend in Heaven--will you not keep vows with Him? Then hear His inviting words, "Return, thou backsliding Israel, saith the Lord, and I will not cause mine anger to fall upon you; for I am merciful, I will not keep anger for ever."--Jer. iii: 12.

2. And have you not still some love for the Saviour, although you have been very unfaithful to Him? Does not your heart desire that He might be loved and honored even by yourself and by all others? Then consider how much reproach your sins cast

upon Him, upon His gospel, and upon His kingdom. Will not men observing your conduct say, 'Ah! here is a subject of the grace of Christ, such grace has little efficacy in saving from sin! Here is exemplified the power of the gospel unto salvation. Indeed it has little power to convert a man from sin! Here is an example from the kingdom of Christ; indeed that kingdom Las little influence in checking sin! And has not Christ said to His disciples "Ye are my witnesses?" What a sad testimony does your sinful life offer concerning Him! From your testimony, surely men would conclude that religion is worthless; that Christ does not by His salvation deliver from the love and power of sin. Oh, what a false witness is that! What reproach, what dishonor is this upon His name! Will not a love for His precious name and a regard for His honor prevail with you to forsake sin? Compare your conduct with that of one who loved the honor of his country Regulus a Roman general, was captured by the Carthagenians. By them, he was sent to Rome to adjust a peace. In case of failure, he was bound by oath to return to Carthage and threatened with cruel tortures. But the terms proposed by the Carthagenians were dishonorable to Rome and Regulus was foremost in denouncing them. Therefore, he returned to

Carthage and suffered death by having spikes driven through his body which was confined in a barrel. You are a soldier in the kingdom of Christ, a kingdom infinitely more worthy to be honored by you than was Rome to be honored by its soldiers. Christ has done more for you than Rome could do for the noblest of her generals. Regulus would not for his life wound his country; will you for a momentary pleasure in sin wound Him who loved you and gave Himself for you? Regulus would not for his life dishonor Rome; will you for a short indulgence in sin, dishonor Him who redeemed you with His precious blood and made you a child of God? Oh, let not this be done by you! Make no more treaties with sin! No more dishonor your Savior, His gospel and His church? Rather endure the greatest self-sacrifice, reproach and suffering than yield to temptation. Be a Regulus for Christ. You may suppose your influence cannot be very important for good or evil. In this you greatly mistake. What! your influence unimportant and you a Christian--a professed follower of Christ? You occupy a new relation to the unregenerate. They regard you as having felt the power of the gospel and as exemplifying the salvation of Christ; therefore your example is clothed with new power; by a sinful life you will influence them to place a low estimate upon the gospel, for they will perceive that you a Christian, are no better than themselves. What destructive evil will thus be done! Does your influence import but little when it leads souls to perdition? The lamp is a little thing, and in itself of little importance, but when hoisted in a light-house to signal some dangerous shoal, how full of import! While burning, how many vessels warned keep safely to the channel or out to the sea! But if that light go out, what noble ships and how many precious lives are wrecked in the breakers! Thus your example, while not professing Christianity, had little influence inducing men either to seek or neglect the salvation of God; but now that you are esteemed a Christian, men expect to find in you a warning light, if danger indeed be nigh, you are a light-house for the world; can your influence be unimportant? Your example will either by the light of godliness, warn men to seek a Savior or by the darkness of sin lure them into a fatal security until their souls be wrecked in perdition. What! your influence unimportant when by it immortal souls may be thereby seduced into eternal disaster? Alas! how many sinners have by false professors or careless Christians been led to fancy themselves secure, never waking from their dreams till hurried into the presence of God!

3. Again, consider how useful you may be if maintaining a consistent Christian life; so long as your conduct is inconsistent with your profession, usefulness is impossible; you may be potent to do evil but powerless to do good. Your only efficiency will be to dishonor the name of Christ, to wound His people and be a stumbling block for the destruction of sinners. Indeed it were far better for you not to live in the world than to continue a life so injurious by its inconsistency. But if you would be useful your greatest efficiency will consist in a Christian life. Who does not know that example is more powerful than precept? Then let your Christian example daily proclaim a Saviour to mankind. Let His power to save be seen in yourself. Let your renewed life like the healed maniac of Gadara shew to your fellow men "how great things the Lord hath done for thee and hath had compassion on thee," and they will not only marvel, but seek the Physician whose power and grace have been manifested in you.

A gentleman relating his first convictions of sin, said, "Walking alone at evening, I heard a childish voice in prayer. Unseen I drew near, and saw a young girl whom I knew well; she was confessing her sins to God and earnestly asking forgiveness. Oh! thought I, if one so pure and young has need of confession and forgiveness what is my need, who have lived many years only to forget God and sin against Him!" See here the power of Christian example! Is not its feeblest voice like the trumpet blasts of the priests of God about Jericho before which the walled city falls down?

Thus also may you by a Christian conduct, convict of sin and direct to Christ those whom you neither see nor know. The benefits which may be effected simply by a Christian example are incalculable. It speaks with silent power to every beholder. It arrests the eye of a thoughtless sinner, and he reflects thus, "That man has truly been regenerated and saved by Christianity, but I who am so different from him, must surely be in the bonds of inequity. He is surely journeying toward heaven and I alas! must be journeying toward perdition." Through the blessing of God this conviction of sin ripens into conversion and a soul is saved from perdition. Often had this power of Christian example been verified; persecutors have been convicted of sin by martyrs, the sick proprietor by his Christian tenant and the master by his Christian servant. Suppose your Christian conduct draws one sinner to Christ, or recovers one backslider from his erring way, you will have covered a multitude of sins. That soul will be a jewel of immortal lustre in the Redeemer's crown and therefore you will have brought inestimable honor to His name, yet more, that soul will dwell in immortal bliss, and therefore you will have secured to a sinner once lost, more happiness than the wealth and glory of a world could bestow. Yet more, you will have done something, perhaps much, in completing the Redeemer's kingdom. That one may bring others to Christ, and they in turn many others; and thus the blessed work springing from your good example shall never cease, till at the end of time, a multitude of souls shall come home to glory. And thus shall the angels rejoice not only once for the sinner that through you came to repentance, but a thousand times and for a thousand sinners strike their harps giving glory to God for your Christian example.

The smallest means will through the blessing of God effect great results. Leonidas with his faithful band withstood the myriads of Xerxes at the pass of Thermopylee. So you may, with the advantage of a Christian name and a faithful example withstand a host of sinners, and with the blessing of God save many. But remember, that one traitor led the Persians by a pathway to the rear of Leonida's army. That little army was lost, Attica desolated and Athens reduced to ashes. So also will an unfaithful example you treacherously give advantage to the enemies of religion, and then alas; what incalculable evil is done! What dishonor to Christ, what wounding of His church? What ruin of souls!

4. A consistent Christian life is a life of happiness, said Jesus to His disciples, "In me ye shall have peace." And again we learn that Christians have "joy and peace in the Holy Spirit," yea, and that they may even "glory in tribulations." Faithful Christians are indeed the happiest persons in the world, for peace flows into their hearts from heavenly fountains. There is a river the streams whereof shall make glad the city of our God." But it will be vain for a Christian to seek gladness from the polluted waters of a sinful world. Even the unregenerate who love sin and have no pleasure in righteousness cannot find peace in the sins they love. God has doomed them to

disappointment. "There is no peace, saith my God, to the wicked." How much less should the Christian expect happiness in sin, which he really hates, which is distasteful to his highest nature and loathsome to his purest affections! If indeed you delight in worldliness, if you both commit sins and have pleasure in them that do them," you can indeed have no pleasure in works of righteousness. But neither is there happiness for you from any other source. You are in the "gall of bitterness" as truly as in "the bonds of iniquity." You must have a "new heart" ere you can have a happy one. But if you have a new heart, it can never draw happiness from sin. If you love God, can you be happy in offending Him? If you love the Lord Jesus can you be happy in dishonoring Him, wounding His people and betraying His kingdom? If you love the Holy Spirit, can you be happy in grieving Him from your heart? I may appeal to your own experience; have you found happiness while seeking it in worldliness? I know you have not. She was not in the circles of honor or the halls of learning; she was not in the dance or at the card table; far was she from the sparkling bowl, and listened not to the call of profanity. Have you been seeking her in forbidden paths. You should have remembered that Happiness is obedient to

God if you are not--she never treads
forbidden paths or haunts forbidden fruit.
And have you forsaken the heavenly viands
of religion to feed on the debauchees or even
the dainties of sin? I do not wonder that your
comfort in Christian hope is gone and that
you have almost banished hope itself. You
are unhappy; every backslidden Christian is
so. It may be because you are regenerate and
your heart loathes the sins you indulge.
When I see the King's son among enemies
or debased among menials I am not
surprised to find him wretched. The child of
God and citizen of heaven, having tasted the
sweetness of peace in Christ can be only
wretched when feeding on the husks of sin.
Therefore break off your sins and return to
Christ the Shepherd of your soul and He will
lead you to green pastures and beside still
waters. Then with a peaceful heart you will
say with David "He restoreth my soul; He
leaded me in the paths of righteousness for
His name's sake; yea, though I walk through
the valley of the shadow of death, I will foar
no evil, for Thou art with me. Thy rod and
Thy staff they comfort me. Thou preparest a
table before me in the presence of mine
enemies. Thou anointest my head with oil,
my cup runneth over."--Psalm xxviii.

71

In the proportion of your faithfulness to Christ will be your happiness as also your usefulness. "The joy of the Lord will be your strength," also for greater usefulness, and your usefulness will in turn exhilarate your joy anew. What pure and exalted happiness is awarded even in this life to faithful discipleship let the following example attest. The happiest person whom God has ever permitted me to see was an old negro man who lived in the town of A. His name was Godfrey. All external circumstances were such as would have conspired, had he not been a Christian, to his misery; and yet no Christian could converse with him without feeling more of emulation than pity. On one of his limbs below the knee on incurable and loathsome sore was eating away his life. He was a freed man and entirely dependent on charities for the necessaries of life; he was living when I first saw him in a room so broken in the roof that not even his couch was secured from the rain. Yet his face was radiant with a sweet and pleasant smile. With emotion he thanked God for putting it into any heart to come to see him. He would not talk of his pains or his poverty except to offset them with the greater blessings of God; and he foiled me in several efforts which I made to direct the conversation to his sufferings. He seemed to realize that he only lived, using his own words, "to tell of the goodness of God." I had a servant with me; the old man turned to him and said, "my son, if you only knew what old Godfrey knows, you would be on your knees day and night till you found Jesus! Wait not till to-morrow, Come now while all things in Christ are ready, come!" Often in every day and sometimes at night, his trembling and broken voice was heard singing, praying, shouting and praising God. This was not the occasional but the daily occupation of his life. Rarely could the passer by fail to hear the voice of shouting Godfrey, and should he open the door to see who was there he would find none but Godfrey and his God. In that condition of outward distress and inward glory he had continued for about six years. The sight of him was a more eloquent appeal for Christianity than the most learned effort of the pulpit. No' sinner could behold him without being warned of hell and invited to heaven: No Christian could see him without desiring grace, which dwelt in him: None could see him and forget him. His death was suitable to his life: for the sweetest peace pervaded his heart and mind--it was seen on his face and heard from his lips, so that none who beheld him, could refrain from saying "Oh! that I may die as Godfrey died." The glory to Christ and blessings to men redounding from this noble Christian example can never be adequately known till the day when Christ shall be glorified in His saints and reward them that diligently serve Him.

5. If you live in sin, whatever be your religious profession, you will certainly be lost." Let no man deceive you--he that doeth righteousness is righteous. He that committed sin is of the Devil."--1 John iii: 7, 8. "He that loveth the world, the love of the Father is not in him."--1 John ii: 15. Applying this plain rule to the habitual life, it must be a criterion of rational hope infallible as the word of God. In what degree you indulge sinful actions or cherish sinful feelings, in that degree have you evidence of your lost estate. A "faith that works by love" is the only genuine faith in the gospel: and only as your faith appears in works of love, have you rational hope of a saved estate. Far be it from me to say that a Christian never falls into sin, but it is characteristic of a Christian not to continue habitually in known sin. It is not certain that at any hour he will not fall into sin, but it is certain that from known sin he will repent.

Perhaps you expect to forsake your sins at some future time; but so long as you are willing to remain in sin, overwhelming evidence indicates that you are in the "bond of iniquity" having "neither part nor lot." in the salvation of Christ. Your fall into sin is not so strong a testimony to your sinful estate, as your willingness to remain in your backsliding. For any one may fall into company which is distasteful to himself, but cannot remain therein. And never will men cleave to that for which they have less affection by leaving that for which they have the greater. As to your expectation to repent at some future period, the vilest sinner cherishes a like thought. But this expectation entertained by both does not render it even probable that either will escape the perdition of ungodly men.

You may say 'Surrounding temptations are too strong for my present return.' This may be sadly true, but let it not even suggest that you have received the Spirit of Christ. It is approximate proof of the reverse. Said Christ "Because iniquity shall abound the love of many shall wax cold, but he that endureth to the end, the same shall be saved."--Matthew xxiv: 12, 13. From which it is evident that a spurious faith and a love but superficial, will not long maintain under trial, even the appearance of godliness, which genuine faith will persevere, exhibiting its Christianity through abounding temptations. The ship which cannot stem the perils of the ocean cannot reach the distant harbor. Nor can the mere professor unable to withstand the assaults of sin, ever reach the haven of eternal bliss." Whatever is born of God overcometh the world and this is the victory that overcometh the world, even our faith."--1 John v: 4. Therefore while you remain without a struggle in subjection to worldliness and sin, think not that you have been born of God. Were you a prince of that Royal blood you would not live in such slavery. Rather conclude that you are a servant of sin, "led capture by the devil at his will." But be assured while you cast off the service of Christ before men that He will cast you off before the face of angels.

Be assured that while sinners are stumbling over you into perdition your portion is with "everlasting burnings." But if you be indeed one of the Redeemer's fold you will hearken to His iuvitations.s Saith He "my heep hear my voice." If you will return, the arms of mercy extend as freely to you as to any sinner. He saith "Return, thou backsliding Israel, and I will not cause mine anger to fall upon you, for I am merciful, I will not keep anger for ever."

HOLDING FORTH THE WORD
OF LIFE.

The keeper of the lighthouse at Calais was once boasting to a traveller of the brilliancy of his lantern, which can be seen ten leagues at sea, when the visitor said to him, "What if one of the lights should chance to go out?" "Never; impossible!" he cried, with a sort of consternation at the bare hypothesis. "Sir," said he, pointing to the ocean, "yonder, where nothing can be seen, there are ships going by to all parts of the world. If to-night one of my burners were out, within six months would come a letter-- perhaps from India, perhaps from America, perhaps from some place I never heard of-- saying, that on such a night, at such an hour, the light of Calais burned dim, the watchman neglected his post, and vessels were in danger. Ah, sir, sometimes in the dark nights in stormy weather I look out to sea, and I feel as if the whole world were looking at my light. Go out? burn dim? Oh, never!"

Was the keeper of this lighthouse so vigilant; did he feel so deeply the importance of his work and its responsibility; and shall Christians neglect their light, and suffer it to grow dim--grow

dim when, for need of its bright shining,
some poor soul, struggling amid the waves
of temptation, may be dashed upon the rocks
of destruction? No. "Hold forth the word of
life," This is the way to save souls. "Holding
forth the word of life," says the apostle;
why? "That I may rejoice, in the day of
Christ, that I have not run in vain, nor
labored in vain."

"For sadder sight the eye can know,
  Than proud bark lost, or seaman's woe--
  The shipwreck of the soul."

LITTLE SINS.

BY THE REV. J. C. RYLE, B. A.

Reader never trifle with little sins. A small! leak will sink a great ship, and a small spark will kindle a great fire, and a little allowed sin, in like manner, will ruin an immortal soul. Take my advice, and never spare a little sin. Israel was commanded to slay every Canaanite, both great and small. Act on the same principle, and show no mercy to little sins. Well says the book of Canticles, "Take us the foxes, the little foxes, that spoil the vines." Cant. 2:15.

Depend on it, no wicked man ever meant to be so wicked at his first beginnings. But he began with allowing himself some little transgression, and that led on to something greater still, and thus he became the miserable being that he now is.

There are two ways of coming down from the top of a church steeple: one is to jump down, and the other is to come down by the steps; but both will lead you to the bottom. So also there are two ways of going to hell: one is to walk into it with your eyes

79

open--few people do that; the other is to go down by the steps of little sins; and that way, I fear, is too common. Put up with a few little sins, and you will soon want a few more. Even a heathen could say, "Whoever was content with only one sin?" And then your course will be regularly worse and worse every year. Well did Jeremy Taylor describe the progress of sin in a man: "First it startles him, then it becomes pleasing, then easy, then delightful, then frequent, then habitual, then confirmed: then the man is impenitent, then obstinate, then resolves never to repent and then he is damned."

Reader, the devil only wants to get the wedge of a little allowed sin into your hearts, and you will soon be all his own. Never play with fire. Never trifle with little sins.

THE ETERNITY OF MORAL INFLUENCE.

"Who can tell," writes one, "the results of such a fact as these two lines disclose? The Rev. Newman Hall's little book, entitled, 'Come to Jesus,' has just passed through its five hundred and forty-sixth thousand." How extensively, how long, and how loudly will such works speak, and how differently from the productions of such men as Byron, Paine, or Bolingbroke. If any earth-born joys, remarks a modern writer, are admitted as visitants amidst the celestial choirs, the joy that springs from having written saving and sanctifying works, is the sweetest that reaches the hearts of the saved. And if, as we believe, any poignant recollections from this earth reach the memories of the lost, not the least bitter will be the remembrance of having written volumes which are circulated by every library, and sold by every vender, in which the foundations of morality are sapped, and the youth of our world poisoned throughout the whole range of their moral character and future hopes.

THINK.

BY THE REV. J. C. RYLE, B. A.

READER, do you ever think? You have a soul as well as a body.--You must die one day. After death comes judgment. Do you ever think?

Want of thought is one simple reason why thousands lose their souls for ever. They will not consider. They will not look forward. They will not reflect on their latter end, and the certain consequences of their present ways. And at last they find they are damned for want of thinking.

Believe me, this world is not a world in which we can do well without thinking. Least of all can we do well in the matter of our souls. 'Don't think," whispers Satan: he knows that an unconverted heart is like a dishonest tradesman's books, it will not bear close inspection. "Consider your ways," says the word of God--stop and think--consider and be wise.

Well says the Spanish proverb, "Hurry comes of the devil." Just as men sometimes marry in haste, and repent at leisure, so they make mistakes about their souls in a minute, and then suffer for it for years. Just as a bad servant does wrong and then says, "I never gave it a thought" so men run into sin, and then say, "I did not think about it--it did not look like sin." Not look like sin! What would you have? Sin will not come to you saying, "I am sin:" it would do little harm if it did. Sin always seems "good and pleasant and desirable," at the time of commission. Oh, get wisdom, get discretion. Remember the words of Solomon: "Ponder the paths of thy feet, and let thy ways be established." Prov. 4: 26. It is a wise saying of Lord Bacon, "Do nothing rashly. Stay a little, that you may make an end the sooner."

Oh, learn to be thoughtful. Learn to consider what you are doing, and whither you are going. Take time for calm reflection. Commune with your own heart, and be still. Remember my caution. DO NOT BE LOST MERELY FOR WANT OF THOUGHT.